THE 9/11 CONSPIRACY

The Untold Truth of the Dark And Unforgettable Day

David J. Fitch

Table of Contents

INTRODUCTION

People around the world still remember September 11, 2001, as a day of great fear, despair, and determination. A bunch of carefully organized terrorist attacks happened on that awful morning and changed the course of human history forever. The 9/11 attacks made people feel very unsafe and showed that even the strongest countries can be attacked too. To honor the people who died and the important lessons we learned from this event, it is very important to think about its significance even now, more than 20 years later.

On September 11, the busy cities of New York, Washington, D.C., and Shanksville, Pennsylvania had a normal morning with lots of people around. But, soon the world will witness the unimaginable destruction caused by Al-Qaeda. The Pentagon and the Twin Towers were important symbols of American strength and resilience. In a terrible event, four commercial airplanes were turned into deadly weapons. United Airlines Flight 93, which was supposed to hit another famous place, crashed into a field in Pennsylvania because the people on board fought bravely against the hijackers.

Countries were very surprised and couldn't believe what happened. The terrible things that occurred caused a lot of shock and made people everywhere feel upset. Almost 3,000 innocent people died, including citizens from more than 90 different countries. It deeply affected humanity. Many other people were affected by the consequences, and they suffered a lot from the pain and hardship of that day. Families were broken apart and left in pieces.

After the 9/11 attacks, people all around the world came together and showed support and strength. People from different areas helped and encouraged those affected by the attacks. Many brave people, like emergency workers, firefighters, police officers, etc., risk their lives to save others. This sentence means that even when something really bad happens, people can still be kind and hopeful.

However, the consequences of 9/11 were not just limited to immediate events. It caused big geopolitical changes that led to military actions everywhere, stricter security rules, and a reassessment of relationships between countries. The tragedy led to a new way of fighting terrorism and started conversations about civil rights, monitoring, and finding a good balance between personal freedoms and security.

It's important to remember not only the tragedy that happened on 9/11 but also the important things we learned from it. By building a community that respects and accepts others, we should honor and remember those who have died by trying. We can find the power and motivation to build a better future by recognizing the strength and unity that emerged after a terrible event.

We will study why it happened, what happened right after, what happened in the long term, and what we can learn from this tragic event in our investigation of 9/11. We will navigate through the complicated story of what happened on September 11th and its lasting impact. By doing this, we show respect to the people who were hurt and we want to create a future that is calm and includes everyone.

Chapter 1: SEPTEMBER 11, 2001

The September 11 attacks, also called the 9/11 attacks, were a set of airplane hijackings and bombings by 19 extremists connected to the Islamic extremist group al-Qaeda. These attacks happened in 2001, targeting American places. These were the most extreme and harmful attacks ever to happen on American soil. The harmful incidents that occurred in New York City and Washington, D.C. caused a lot of damage and destruction and led to a big effort by America to fight against terrorism. A total of 19 bad people called terrorists were killed; 2,750 innocent people died in New York, 184 in the Pentagon, and 40 in Pennsylvania (where one of the stolen planes crashed when the passengers tried to take control of it). Many people went to the place where the attacks happened, and more than 400 police officers and firefighters died in New York, which was really affected by the attacks.

How It Happened

Osama bin Laden, who was in charge of the militant Islamic group al-Qaeda, had wrong beliefs about the United States before the September 11 attacks. His beliefs played a major role in causing those attacks. According to an Egyptian named Abu Walid al-Masri, who interacted with bin Laden in Afghanistan in the 1980s and 1990s, bin Laden became increasingly convinced of America's vulnerability in the years leading up to the attacks. Masri thought that the United States was not as strong as others thought. He pointed to what happened in Beirut when they had to leave because of a bombing and many American soldiers died. Bin Laden believed that the US was weak and easily defeated. This idea came from events like when the US left Lebanon after a big attack when they left Somalia after many soldiers were killed, and when they left Vietnam years ago.

Khalid Sheikh Mohammed is often called "KSM" in reports and the media. He was a person from Kuwait who planned the September 11 attacks. When Khalid Sheikh Mohammed was 16 years old, he joined the Muslim Brotherhood and got involved with it. Afterward, he went to the United States to continue learning and got a degree from North Carolina Agricultural and Technical State University in 1986. After that, he traveled to Pakistan and Afghanistan to fight against the Soviet Union, which had invaded Afghanistan in 1979.

In a 2002 interview with Yosri Fouda on Al Jazeera, Khalid Sheikh Mohammed said that in the mid-1990s, he planned to blow up twelve American planes in Asia. Even though his "Bojinka" plan failed, he still wanted to make it happen. And I think that when he shook hands with bin Laden, he realized that he now had a chance to achieve his long-awaited goal.

In 1996, in Tora Bora, Afghanistan, Khalid Sheikh Mohammed met with bin Laden. The 9-11 Commission was started in 2002 by

President George W. Bush, who served as the president of the United States and helped shape the direction of the country. The Congress is investigating the attacks that happened in 2001. Khalid Sheikh Mohammed suggested a plan where pilots would be trained to crash planes into buildings in the United States. Al-Qaeda gave the people, the materials, and support needed for the operation, while Khalid Sheikh Mohammed created a clever and unique plan to use hijacked planes to attack the United States. Bin Laden included the attacks on New York and Washington in a bigger plan to attack the United States and bring about changes in the Middle Eastern governments.

The September 11th terrorist attack showed that Al-Qaeda had influence all over the world. Meetings were organized in Malaysia, people were taught to fly planes in the United States, the plan was managed by leaders in Hamburg, Germany, money was sent from Dubai, and people willing to give up their lives were recruited from countries in the Middle East. In simpler terms, the leaders of al-Qaeda in

Afghanistan were ultimately in charge of all of these actions.

Important parts of the plan for September 11 were created in Hamburg. In 1999, on a train in Germany, an Islamist militant started talking with four important pilots and planners from the "Hamburg cell". These individuals would later be in charge of the September 11 attacks, and one of them was Mohammed Atta, the main hijacker. They talked about doing a holy war in the Russian region of Chechnya. The terrorist-linked the Hamburg group with a member of al-Qaeda who was in Germany. The al-Qaeda member mentioned that going to Chechnya was hard because many tourists were stuck in Georgia. Instead, he suggested that they should travel to Afghanistan.

Even though Afghanistan was important for al-Qaeda's development, the plotters' experience in the Western countries provided them with the necessary abilities to carry out the attacks and also increased their excitement. While living in Hamburg, three out of the four people who planned to hijack planes on

September 11, along with one of the main organizers named Ramzi Binalshibh, became more and more extreme in their beliefs. They have all become more extreme because they feel lonely, miss their home, and believe they are being treated unfairly. They started to separate themselves from the outside world and became more extreme in their beliefs. Eventually, they decided to join bin Laden's fight and went to Afghanistan to join al-Qaeda in 1999.

Atta and his friends from Hamburg went to Afghanistan in 1999, right when the September 11 plan was being prepared. Atta and his fellow jihadists who were educated in the West were more capable of leading the attacks in Washington and New York than the soldiers they had recruited before. This is why bin Laden and his military commander Muhammad Atef chose Atta to lead the operation.

The hijackers, most of them from Saudi Arabia, came to live in the US, and many of them arrived there long before the attacks took place. A few of them formed small groups and had instructions on how to fly commercially.

Atta used email to tell Binalshibh about how the plan was progressing while he was in the US. Atta used secret coding in the messages, pretending to be talking to his fiancée "Jenny," to tell Binalshibh that they were almost finished with their training and ready for the attacks. In one message, Atta said, "The first semester starts in three weeks. We have to take four tests and get nineteen private education certificates. The four "exams" were the things that were attacked. The 19 "certificates" were special codes that showed who the 19 hijackers from al-Qaeda were.

On August 29, 2001, in the early morning, Atta asked Binalshibh a riddle: "Two sticks, a dash, and a cake with a stick down—what is it? " After thinking about it, Binalshibh figured out that Atta meant the attacks would happen in two weeks. The two sticks meant 11 and the cake with a stick down meant 9. The information showed that the attacks would happen on September 11. In most other countries, the day before the month is used in numeric dates, but in the United States, it is the opposite. So, in the

United States, it was 9-11 instead of 11-9. Binalshibh left Germany and went to Pakistan on September 5th. After reaching the destination, he sent a messenger to Afghanistan to inform bin Laden about when and how big the attack would be.

The Attacks

On September 11, 2001, a bunch of bad people got on four planes at three airports on the East Coast. After the plane took off, the hijackers made the staff unable to do anything by possibly using box cutters to hurt them. The very big planes with lots of fuel that were flying towards the West Coast were taken control of by the hijackers. The first plane that crashed into the World Trade Center in New York City was American Airlines Flight 11. It departed from Boston at 8:46 AM. At first, most people thought that this was a small plane accident. Seventeen minutes later, the plane from United Airlines that came from Boston crashed into the southern tower.

There was no doubt that the United States was being attacked at that time. The crash caused a lot of damage to all the buildings, and they also started burning. A few office workers who were trapped higher up in the buildings decided to jump out to save themselves instead of staying and getting hurt by the fires that were burning inside the tall buildings. At 9:37 AM, a plane from American Airlines crashed into the side of the Pentagon, causing a fire. The crash happened near Washington, D.C., outside the city. The fourth airplane, United Airlines Flight 93 from Newark, New Jersey, crashed near Shanksville in Pennsylvania within an hour (at 10:03 AM) after the people onboard, who were informed about the situation through their cell phones, tried to fight against the people attacking them. A little while later, the Federal Aviation Authority said that all planes in the country had to stop flying.

The broken south tower of the World Trade Center fell down at 9:59 AM, and the north tower fell down 29 minutes later. The streets in Lower Manhattan quickly became covered with smoke and debris. Office workers and people who live nearby escaped in fear as they hurriedly tried to run away from the increasing clouds of debris. Buildings near the Twin Towers were badly damaged, and a few of them fell down later on. Fires burned at the World Trade Center site for over three months.

As people across the country and the world tried to understand how many people were hurt or killed, rescuers quickly began trying to save lives. Almost 3,000 people lost their lives, which includes all 19 terrorists and 2,750 victims in New York, 184 in the Pentagon, and 40 in Pennsylvania. Over 400 police officers and firemen who died after going quickly to the place and into the buildings were counted as part of the overall number in New York City.

In a second-grade class in Sarasota, Florida, on the morning of September 11, President Bush found out that a plane had crashed into the World Trade Center. The president's chief of staff, Andrew Card, crouched down and quietly said to the president, "Another plane hit the other tower. " The United States is being attacked. To make sure the president was safe, Bush flew Air Force One back and forth all over the country. In the end, he landed in Washington, D.C. C in the evening after the attacks. At 8:30 p.m., Bush gave a speech to the country from the Oval Office. He explained an important part of his administration's upcoming foreign policy: "We will treat all terrorists and the countries that support them the same. "

On September 14, Bush visited "Ground Zero," the burning location where the World Trade Center was destroyed and many people lost their lives. Bush climbed onto a broken fire truck and grabbed a loudspeaker to talk to the people trying really hard to find anyone who was still alive. Bush's strong response to the attacks made more people like him. His approval rating went from 55% before September 11 to 90% shortly after, which is the highest ever recorded for a president.

Chapter 2: The Aftermath Of The Attack

The attacks, especially the collapse of the Twin Towers, which was the most well-known building in New York City, caused a lot of emotional pain. The World Trade Center was in the middle of a very big city. This was different from Pearl Harbor in 1941, which was in a more secluded place. The September 11 events were compared to the attack on Pearl Harbor. Lots of people took pictures and videos of the attacks and many others watched it happening on TV. After September 11, videos of the attacks and pictures of sad people at "Ground Zero" (the area where the Twin Towers used to be) were shown a lot on TV. The pictures showed family members who were missing, hoping to find out what happened to them.

Also, the global economy was greatly harmed. The buildings in the middle of New York's financial area were damaged, so the stock markets in New York stopped for four days.

People were concerned that this might cause a big problem in the stock market. After that, markets saw very big losses. The attacks caused many passengers to be stuck in different parts of the country. Commercial flights were not allowed to fly in American airspace until September 13th, and it took several days for flights to go back to normal with tighter security measures.

Al-Qaeda had a very successful plan with the September 11 attacks. The attacks became much bigger because they were shown on TV and seen by millions of people all over the world. The attacks were well-planned and targeted important places of the enemy. The act of spreading information about the event that happened on September 11th was done in a very public way through the media. This made sure that a lot of people knew about it. Many people from all over the world have not witnessed a terrorist attack happening live since the time when Israeli athletes were taken hostage and killed during the Munich Olympics in 1972, while they were watching it on television. Al-Qaeda was not very well-known before September 11, but after that, it became famous.

The French newspaper Le Monde wrote a headline saying that everyone is now united with Americans after the September 11 attacks. This sentiment was echoed by American allies. In Tehran, the capital of Iran, hundreds of people gathered for a candlelight vigil.

Many countries believed the Americans when they showed evidence that al-Qaeda, a group of Islamic terrorists, was responsible for the attacks. The group had been connected to previous violent attacks on Americans, and bin Laden had frequently shown his dislike for the United States. Al-Qaeda's main base was in Afghanistan, where it had formed a strong bond with the Taliban militia that controlled the country. Because of this, the Taliban militia refused to hand over bin Laden to the Americans and to halt al-Qaeda's activities in that area.

NATO used Article 5 for the first time ever. This allowed its members to work together to protect themselves. On October 7, the United States and its allies attacked Afghanistan. In a short time, many terrorists from al-Qaeda and Taliban were either killed or caught, which made their leaders hide from the authorities. The US government focused on fighting terrorism as the main goal of its foreign policy. They worked hard to locate more al-Qaeda members and their supporters worldwide. At that time, security got much stronger in the United States at places like airports, government buildings, and sports events.

The USA PATRIOT Act, which was passed in 2001, gave the FBI and other law-enforcement agencies more power to search and spy on people in order to fight terrorism. It was passed quickly to help with the response to terrorism inside the country. A Department of Homeland Security was created with a high-ranking position in the government.

The September 11 attacks didn't work out well for al-Qaeda, even though they caused a lot of damage and killed many people. Al-Qaeda, which means "the base" in Arabic, lost its strongest place in Afghanistan after September 11. Some al-Qaeda leaders tried to say that the

Western involvement in Afghanistan was a success for al-Qaeda, even though some of them had originally disagreed with the attacks. During an interview four years later, Al-Adel, who was one of the group's military leaders, shared that the attacks on New York and Washington were part of a plan to provoke the United States into making unwise decisions.

But, there is no evidence to support the idea that the al-Qaeda leaders were thinking about an American invasion of Afghanistan before September 11, 2001. They left their training areas to be prepared for possible attacks from the United States by air or with missiles. Additionally, it is uncertain that the Taliban's downfall was an error made by America, considering that it resulted in the destruction of the only government in the modern Muslim world that followed al-Qaeda's strict rules. This also led to the loss of an entire nation, which used to serve as a safe space for the organization. Al-Qaeda couldn't regain its power and control over Afghanistan after the Taliban were removed.

Bin Laden made a mistake in underestimating the power of the United States. Attempting to simplify: People's reactions to the September 11 attacks were misguided. They believed it meant the United States would withdraw from the Middle East, similar to what happened in 1993. To put it simply, withdrawing from Somalia or repeating a round of missile attacks, similar to the ones that happened after the bombings in 1998. al-Qaeda attacked the embassies in Kenya and Tanzania. These two things did not happen as we expected.

soldiers, the Taliban government in Afghanistan was overthrown in 2001. The Northern Alliance, a group of Afghan fighters, worked together with the United States to remove the Taliban from power. The United States used Special Forces soldiers and CIA officers to fight against the Taliban. Two months after the September 11 attacks, in November, the Northern Alliance and the US removed the Taliban from power. However, the United States was still at the beginning of what would become its longest war. Their goal was to prevent the Taliban and al-Qaeda from coming back.

In December 2001, the government decided to keep prisoners at Guantánamo Bay. This place had been rented by the United States from Cuba since 1903. They made this choice because they needed a location to keep the prisoners after the Taliban fell. Donald Rumsfeld, who was in charge of defense, said on December 27, 2001, that Guantánamo Bay in Cuba was not a perfect place but it was the best option available. The people in charge of the government liked Guantánamo because it was far away from American laws, so the prisoners couldn't argue that they were being held unfairly, but it was still close to Florida so it was easy for government agencies to go there, and get information from the hundreds of dangerous terrorists they believed were there. In simpler words, currently, there are around 800 prisoners staying there. However, on the 10th anniversary of the September 11 attacks, there were less than 175 inmates.

In a speech on January 29, 2002, President Bush talked about a new idea for starting a war called preemptive war. This idea was different from what most people believed, as it meant that the US could start a war even before an enemy attacked if it thought that the enemy could harm the country. Bush announced

Iran, Iraq, and North Korea were grouped together by Bush and called the "axis of evil" because he believed these governments were very dangerous. Bush talked about his theory of starting a war before being attacked by the group of West Point cadets and their families at the graduation ceremony on June 1, 2002. He said that if we wait for threats to become real, it will be too late. Bush believed that removing Saddam Hussein's government in Iraq would show others not to attack the United States.

So, even though there was no evidence showing that Saddam Hussein's administration in Iraq was involved in the September 11 attacks, the United States got ready to fight against Iraq as part of its bigger fight against terrorism around the world.

On March 19, 2003, President Bush ordered the start of the war, just a few days before the attack on Iraq.

The war in Iraq led by the United States began on March 20th. In just three weeks, American soldiers had gained control of Baghdad. The world witnessed the famous images of Saddam Hussein's threatening monument being pulled down from its foundation.

Bin Laden's Pursuit

In September 2001, President Bush said that he wanted Osama bin Laden to be either killed or caught. As a result, a reward of $25 million was eventually offered for any information that would lead to bin Laden's death or capture. However, even in December 2001, when American soldiers went after him to the Tora Bora mountains in the east of Afghanistan, Bin Laden was able to avoid being captured. After a pause in the investigation, it was thought that

Bin Laden was living in the tribal regions of Pakistan and Afghanistan.

United Intelligence finally found him in Pakistan, where he was living in Abbottabad, a city with many military bases. The US gave directions to President Barack Obama, along with a small group of American individuals. On May 2, 2011, a group of Navy SEALs forcefully entered his building and shot and killed the leader of al-Qaeda.

After the War in Afghanistan began, Osama bin Laden, who started al-Qaeda and used to lead it, hid to avoid being caught by the United States or its friends. He hid because he was part of the 9/11 attacks in 2001 and had been on the FBI's most wanted list since 1999. We didn't know where he was after he escaped arrest in the Battle of Tora Bora in December 2001. There were many rumors about his health, whether he was still working with al-Qaeda, and where he was. At that time, Bin Laden also made many recordings on audio and video.

The US government tried really hard to find bin Laden for ten years after he disappeared. General Stanley McChrystal is a high-ranking military leader from the United States. The Army stated in December 2009 that it was necessary to either catch or kill bin Laden for the United States. The aim is to ultimately overcome al-Qaeda.

American intelligence agents found out where Osama bin Laden was because they tracked one of the people who delivered things for him. The people held at Guantánamo Bay gave intelligence officials valuable information. They told them the name the courier used, which was Abu Ahmed al-Kuwaiti. Al-Kuwaiti was discovered to be living in Abbottabad, Pakistan, in 2009. In August 2010, Al-Kuwaiti was discovered and traced to the Abbottabad complex. This made CIA paramilitary agents think that bin Laden was hiding there.

On May 1, 2011, President Barack Obama told a group of special Navy fighters, known as the Navy SEALs, to attack the complex. Bin Laden was shot two times during the 40-minute raid.

One bullet hit his chest and the other hit above his left eye. The SEALs beat and killed the rest of the people in the building complex. Bin Laden's body was taken out of the building, together with computer hard drives, papers, and other things.

Chapter 3: The Unanswered Questions

The really sad things that happened on September 11, 2001, completely changed history and stayed in everyone's minds. We need to understand more about the details and complexities of 9/11 as the 20th anniversary of the tragic event approaches. People are still bringing up questions and concerns about the attacks and what happened afterward. Many aspects of the attacks have been carefully examined, but there are still some questions that haven't been answered, which makes people unsure and demands more study. This investigation aims to dig deeper into the unanswered questions about 9/11, urging us to think about the missing information and encouraging ongoing discussions in our quest for the truth.

Doubts, contradictions, and real-life events have been around since the start, leading to skepticism and different ideas. The information about the attacks is still a mystery. How were the terrorists with box cutters able to get past security and hijack planes? How did they carry out a coordinated attack on multiple locations, targeting important American symbols?

There are different opinions about why the World Trade Center towers collapsed. The reason given by the authorities is that the intense heat from the jet fuel caused damage to the structure of the buildings. However, some people have raised doubts about the way the buildings fell, which was not typical. These people who don't believe it question whether the collapse was only caused by the planes crashing into the buildings and the resulting fires. They suggest other ideas like planned demolitions or different reasons for why the buildings were destroyed.

Furthermore, there are worries about mistakes and possible early information about the attacks. Did the United States know about something that could have prevented the tragedy? They didn't pay attention to or take the warnings seriously enough. People are talking and complaining about how intelligence agencies are involved in things and how the government is reacting to it.

Moreover, there are still many unanswered worries about what happened after 9/11 and the military actions led by the United States in Afghanistan and Iraq. People are still discussing and studying the reasons behind these military operations, how trustworthy the information that was used is, and what impact they will have in the future. Some people are unsure if the actions taken after 9/11 have actually made the world safer or if they have unknowingly caused more instability and violence.

Although there are still many unanswered questions, various inquiries, like the 9/11 Commission Report, have provided valuable information about what happened on that specific day. These investigations have helped us make our country safer and prevent terrorism in the future. They have also given us more information about the attacks and the people who were involved in them. The fact that there are still questions without answers and different opinions shows that we should keep reviewing, investigating, and talking openly about them.

It is important to remember and show respect for the people who were hurt or killed, their families, and the strong unity of the community during a difficult time as we commemorate the 20th anniversary of 9/11. At the same time, we must keep working hard to find solutions, encourage openness, and have smart conversations that could help us understand this important time in history better. We try our best to uphold the importance of getting things right, being fair, and being fully committed to learning from history in order to make the present better. We do this by acknowledging and addressing the problems that still need to be resolved.

Here are a few of the questions that still don't have answers about the events of 9/11:

1. **Attack on the Pentagon:** Some people do not believe the official story of how American Airlines Flight 77 crashed into

the Pentagon. Doubters argue that the damage to the building couldn't have been caused by an airplane accident. They suggest that a missile or explosive device may have been responsible.

2. Some people think that explosive demolitions caused the World Trade Center towers (WTC 1, 2, and 7) to collapse, instead of the planes crashing into them and the resulting fires. They claim that the buildings collapsed in a way that suggests they were intentionally brought down using controlled demolitions.

3. Insider trading is when someone trades stocks based on secret information. It is alleged that there was suspicious trading before 9/11, suggesting that someone knew about the attacks and used this information to make money. Thorough investigations have not found any strong evidence to support these accusations.

4. After the United Airlines Flight 93 disaster in Pennsylvania, people have come up with conspiracy theories. Some people say that the jet was hit by a missile or purposely shot down to stop it from going to its intended destination, possibly the White House or the United States. The Capitol is the building where government leaders meet and make important decisions.

It is important to mention again that detailed investigations, such as the one done by the 9/11 Commission in 2004, have provided explanations for these events, resolved many of the unresolved problems, and proved that several conspiracy theories are false. People who know a lot about certain jobs, like building structures, and airplanes, and gathering information, really support the official reasons given for what happened.

The Historical Precedents

Although the events of September 11, 2001, were unique and had a big impact, we can look at similar things that happened in the past to understand what led to 9/11. It is important to remember that these examples show how things have happened in the past and are not exact comparisons. These examples contributed to the conditions that led to the 9/11 attacks. Here are some important historical examples:

1. Islamic Extremism and Terrorism: Both the rise of radical Islamic beliefs and the use of terrorism for political and ideological goals have roots in the past. Extremist groups like al-Qaeda have been influenced by the ideas and actions of past beliefs and movements. For example, during the 1900s, extreme Muslim groups got their ideas from people like Sayyid Qutb, who taught a strong Muslim belief and encouraged violence. We can better understand why the 9/11 attacks happened by looking at previous historical events.

2. The History of American Intervention in the Middle East: The United States' history of involvement in the Middle East has greatly impacted the region and shaped the political landscape in which the 9/11 attacks occurred. The war between the Soviet Union and Afghanistan, the conflict in the Gulf in 1990-1991, and events like the revolution in Iran in 1979 affected how the Middle East operated. Extremist groups took advantage of a dislike for America that was fueled by the US support of harsh governments, military actions, and political interests in the region.

3. Terrorist assaults on U.S. Targets: Before the September 11th attacks, there were numerous severe acts of terrorism in the United States. Extremist groups' ability to carry out attacks in our country was demonstrated by specific targets. For example, the bombing of the World Trade Center in 1993, done by people connected to extremist Islamic groups, showed that famous American landmarks can be easily damaged and suggested the threat of worldwide terrorism.

4. Terrorism's Changing Nature: By the end of the 20th century, terrorism started to become different. More and more terrorist groups are using transnational strategies, which means they are attacking people in different countries. Organizations like al-Qaeda were able to work in different countries, plan big attacks, and recruit people from other nations because new communication and transportation technology helped create global networks.

5. Security and Intelligence Challenges: In the past, there have been times when problems with security and intelligence have made it hard to stop and respond to terrorist attacks. The USS Cole and the United States were attacked. In 1998, there were attacks on embassies in Kenya and Tanzania, and in 2000, the USS Cole was bombed. These incidents showed that there were problems with how different agencies coordinated, shared, and collected information. These mistakes made it clear that it is very important to improve efforts against terrorism and make changes to the intelligence community.

The events of 9/11 become easier to understand when we consider similar events that have happened before. Let me explain clearly, Every event in history has its own special circumstances and details. The events of 9/11 were a major moment that influenced what happened next, like policies, security, and relationships between countries. These events also led to important changes in the world.

Chapter 4: The 9/11 Backlash

The attacks that happened on September 11, 2001, also known as 9/11, were a set of carefully planned terrorist actions by the group called al-Qaeda. They targeted the United States. These attacks had a big impact on many parts of society, both in our country and other countries. The response to the events of 9/11 was one of the significant outcomes. This reaction had many different parts, such as politics, society, money, and culture. In this response, we will look at each of these parts and give a detailed analysis of the reaction to the 9/11 event.

1. Political Backlash: After the September 11 attacks, there was a strong negative reaction in politics that resulted in many changes to laws in both the United States and other countries. George W. is a person's name. President Bush from the United States started a campaign called the "War on Terror". The aims of

Al-Qaeda were to break things apart and prevent terrorist attacks around the world. The USA PATRIOT Act was created to give the government more power to monitor, collect information, and enforce the law. It was approved by the US Congress because of the attacks that happened. These rules caused arguments and raised concerns about people's rights and privacy.

Countries from around the world began a military mission in Afghanistan to remove the Taliban government, as they had allowed al-Qaeda to seek safety there. The invasion of Iraq in 2003 caused a lot of disagreement because some people believed it was necessary to fight terrorism and stop the country from having weapons of mass destruction (WMD). These military actions caused a long and costly war in both countries and were criticized by many different sources.

2. Social Backlash: After 9/11, there was a negative reaction from people in society. This led to more unfair treatment, unfair judgment, and unfair actions based on a person's race or religion. After the attacks, there were more instances of hate crimes and crimes targeting people believed to be Muslim or from the Middle East. Mosques were destroyed, and Muslims were watched more closely, which made them feel scared and left out. Sikh Americans were also affected by people's reactions because they were often mistaken for Muslims due to their appearance and experienced hate crimes too.

3. Economic Backlash: The economic consequences of 9/11 were really bad, especially for the industries that were directly affected by the attacks. The airline industry was badly hurt by a big decrease in air travel and the money they lost because of it. Airlines had to make big changes and spend more money on security because of new laws. Additionally, because people were afraid to travel due to safety concerns, tourism also decreased, especially in large parts of the United States. Cities are places where many people live together. They have buildings, houses, and streets. The attacks also caused bigger problems for the economy, which contributed to a decrease in the world economy.

4. Cultural Backlash: After 9/11, people reacted strongly against different aspects of culture, which led to changes in how the media portrayed things, how people talked about things in public, and how they felt towards Islam. The attacks made people more anxious and suspicious of Muslims. This led to wrong information and unfair judgment in the media. As more people hold negative beliefs and spread conspiracy theories about Islam and Muslims, the fear and hatred towards them, known as Islamophobia, is becoming more common. Movies, TV shows, and books started featuring the Middle East and terrorism more frequently because people were reacting to the culture. This also affected the arts and entertainment industry.

After the 9/11 attacks, there were many consequences that lasted a long time. However, people did not all react in the same way. Many people and groups worked hard to fight against unfair treatment and hatred and also promoted understanding, acceptance, and communication among different religions. It was realized that we should not judge or harm entire groups of people because of the actions of a few extremists. So, steps were taken to stop the unfair treatment of Muslims and encourage acceptance.

How We Remember

For people who were affected by the attacks - individuals, groups, and countries - remembering 9/11 is very significant. This serves as a sad reminder of the victims' deaths, the bravery of the first responders, and the ongoing impact on society. Below is a detailed overview of how people remember the events of September 11th, 2001.

1. **Anniversary Remembrances:** On the anniversary of the attacks on September 11, people around the world, but especially in the US, hold memorial services and rituals to remember the event. The National September

11 Memorial & Museum in New York City is a place where the Twin Towers used to be. It is very important and hosts a significant ceremony. People who survived, people who came to help, government workers and families of the people who died come together to show respect, stay quiet, read the names of the people who died and think about what the day means.

2. Memorials & Monuments: To honor and remember the people who were harmed or killed, special places like memorials and monuments have been created. The National September 11 Memorial & Museum is a very famous place that has big pools where the Twin Towers used to be, and also a museum that tells the story of what happened on September 11 and what happened after. There are many important monuments in different cities and states. Examples include the Pentagon Memorial in Arlington, Virginia, and the Empty Sky Memorial at Liberty State Park, New Jersey.

3. Survivor testimony and Personal tales: To keep the memory of 9/11 alive, people who survived the attacks or were harmed by them share their stories and experiences. These personal stories help us understand the events better and remind us of the strength, bravery, and care shown by people before and after the attacks. These accounts help future generations understand the true cost of tragedy and the importance of unity within a community.

4. Educational Initiatives and Museums: Museums and educational programs are both important in remembering and sharing information about 9/11. To help people understand and learn about history, we do things like educational programs, talks, displays, and online resources. They also encourage discussions about how the events of 9/11 have influenced politics, security, and other aspects of society.

5. International Remembrance: The whole world remembers the events of 9/11, not just the United States. The attacks affected the whole world, causing changes in how countries fight against terrorism, make decisions about security, and handle conflicts in different areas.

Many countries express their support for the United States and honor the victims of 9/11 through ceremonies, quiet moments, and symbolic gestures. The world's collective fight against terrorism and promotion of peace is highlighted by the response to the events of 9/11.

6. Acts of Service and remembering: On September 11th, individuals and groups take part in informal acts of service and remembrance along with public ceremonies. This means helping the community by volunteering, participating in charitable activities, and doing good things as a way to honor the spirit of working together and recovering after the attacks. These actions show how 9/11 still affects society and people's commitment to moving forward.

Remembering 9/11 happens in different ways, like special events, personal stories, special places, learning activities, and helpful actions. The impact of 9/11 continues to be remembered through many events that promote

self-reflection, strength, and a commitment to
unity and kindness in challenging times.

Chapter 5: Conclusion

First, 9/11 was a really sad event where more than 3,000 innocent people lost their lives. The day will always be remembered by everyone who witnessed the terrible event. This is a sad reminder of how strong hate can be and how harmful fanaticism can be. We must always remember the people who were hurt, their families, and the brave actions of the first responders who risked their own lives to save others.

Many different places went through big changes because of 9/11. The attacks made the United States start the "War on Terror" campaign. This led to military actions in Afghanistan and Iraq. These actions tried to dismantle groups of terrorists, bring about peace, and prevent future attacks. However, they also started conversations, negative comments, and complicated effects on global relationships that still matter in the world today.

The events of 9/11 caused a lot of prejudice and fear towards Muslims, which made them feel excluded from society. It is important to know that terrorists are usually extremists and should not be connected with one religion or its followers. To promote inclusivity and reduce the negative effects of the aftermath of the attacks, it is still important to work hard to eliminate prejudice and increase understanding.

The events of 9/11 had a big impact on the economy, especially for industries that were directly affected by the attacks. The global economy went through a bad time with big losses in the aviation and tourist industries. But when individuals, cities, and businesses joined forces to recover and reconstruct, their determination and persistence emerged victoriously.

After 9/11, there were many tough conversations about how Islam and terrorism are shown in the media and popular culture. These talks also brought up questions about identity and representation. It is important to learn in detail and change your ideas about Muslim communities because they are diverse and can be found all around the world.

In simple words: 9/11 was a very important event that had a big impact on history in many different ways. This event made us realize how important it is for countries to work together, be strong, and understand, and showed us that even powerful countries can be vulnerable. We have a responsibility to keep the memories of the victims alive by promoting unity, empathy, and calmness. We can work towards a future where talking and understanding beat fear and division by learning from the lessons of 9/11 and taking them seriously.